A TALE OF TWO CITIES

by

Charles Dickens

Adapted by

Everett Quinton

Originally Produced by The Ridiculous Theatrical
Company of New York City

SAMUEL FRENCH, INC.
45 WEST 25th STREET   NEW YORK 10010
7623 SUNSET BOULEVARD   HOLLYWOOD 90046
LONDON   *TORONTO*

Copyright © 1990 by Everett Quinton

ALL RIGHTS RESERVED

CAUTION: Professionals and amateurs are hereby warned that A TALE OF TWO CITIES is subject to a royalty. It is fully protected under the copyright laws of the United States of America, the British Commonwealth, including Canada, and all other countries of the Copyright Union. All rights, including professional, amateur, motion pictures, recitation, lecturing, public reading, radio broadcasting, television, and the rights of translation into foreign languages are strictly reserved. In its present form the play is dedicated to the reading public only.

The amateur live stage performance rights to A TALE OF TWO CITIES are controlled exclusively by Samuel French, Inc., and royalty arrangements and licenses must be secured well in advance of presentation. PLEASE NOTE that amateur royalty fees are set upon application in accordance with your producing circumstances. When applying for a royalty quotation and license please give us the number of performances intended, dates of production, your seating capacity and admission fee. Royalties are payable one week before the opening performance of the play to Samuel French, Inc., at 45 W. 25th Street, New York, NY 10010; or at 7623 Sunset Blvd., Hollywood, CA 90046, or to Samuel French (Canada), Ltd., 80 Richmond Street East, Toronto, Ontario, Canada M5C 1P1.

Royalty of the required amount must be paid whether the play is presented for charity or gain and whether or not admission is charged.

Stock royalty quoted on application to Samuel French, Inc.

For all other rights than those stipulated above, apply to Walter Gidaly, Esq., Moldover, Hertz, Presnick & Gidaly, 750 Third Avenue, New York, NY 10017.

Particular emphasis is laid on the question of amateur or professional readings, permission and terms for which must be secured in writing from Samuel French, Inc.

Copying from this book in whole or in part is strictly forbidden by law, and the right of performance is not transferable.

Whenever the play is produced the following notice must appear on all programs, printing and advertising for the play: "Produced by special arrangement with Samuel French, Inc."

Due authorship credit must be given on all programs, printing and advertising for the play.

ISBN 0 573 69190 8   Printed in U.S.A.

IMPORTANT BILLING AND CREDIT REQUIREMENTS

All producers of A TALE OF TWO CITIES *must* give credit to the Adaptor of the Play in all programs distributed in connection with performances of the Play and in all instances in which the title of the Play appears for purposes of advertising, publicizing or otherwise exploiting the Play and/or a production. The name of the Adaptor *must* also appear on a separate line, on which no other name appears, immediately following the title, and *must* appear in size of type not less than fifty percent the size of the title type.

The billing of the Adaptor shall appear in programs or playbills as it has appeared in the playbill of The Ridiculous Theatrical Company's New York City presentation of the Play, as follows:

(Name of Producer)
presents
A TALE OF TWO CITIES
by
Charles Dickens
Adapted by
Everett Quinton
Originally Produced by THE RIDICULOUS THEATRICAL
COMPANY of New York City

No one shall commit or authorize any act or omission by which the copyright of, or the right to copyright, this play may be impaired.

No one shall make any changes in this play for the purpose of production.

Publication of this play does not imply availability for performance. Both amateurs and professionals considering a production are *strongly* advised in their own interests to apply to Samuel French, Inc., for written permission before starting rehearsals, advertising, or booking a theatre.

No part of this book may be reproduced, stored in a retrieval system, or transmitted in any form, by any means, now known or yet to be invented, including mechanical, electronic, photocopying, recording, videotaping, or otherwise, without the prior written permission of the publisher.

Note: *A Tale of Two Cities* is a solo performance. Character names refer to the characters played by JERRY, the play's protagonist.

Setting: A studio apartment in lower Manhattan.

Time: Present.

A TALE OF TWO CITIES was first performed in New York City in July 1989 at The Charles Ludlam Theater (The Ridiculous Theatrical Company) with the following cast and crew:

JERRY...Everett Quinton

Director..Kate Stafford
Set ....Jan Bell, James Eckerle, Daphne Groos
Costumes.. Susan Young
Lights ....Richard Currie

A Tale of Two Cities

SETTING: A tiny studio apartment in lower Manhattan, entrance up right, a convertible sofa stage center, a combination dresser/bookcase crammed with knicknacks upstage center, a coat rack up left, a dressing table and chair stage left, shelves on wall with wigs and hats, a closet offstage left, a window barred by a window guard upstage right, a small utility kitchen up right, and a bathtub stage right.

AT RISE: Ponytailed JERRY enters, laden with packages. HE drops a grocery bag by the kitchen, kisses and humps a clothes box, opens the closet, from which a great deal of junk pours out, kicks the contents back into the closet, tosses in the remainder of this packages, takes off and hangs up his denim, lace, and leather jacket, is startled by himself in the mirror on the back of the closet door, kisses his reflection when HE recognizes it, closes the closet, checks his mail, saves electric bill, drops rest in garbage, unloads his groceries onto the kitchen shelves and into the small refrigerator, opens a can of soda, opens a package of donuts and takes one, examines the donut carefully, sits on his sofa, heaves a sigh of relief, and sips his soda.

JERRY. Shit! (*Puts the soda down on a kitchen shelf, crosses to the telephone on his dressing table, dials, waits impatiently through the message on an answering machine.*) Hi Mary-Margaret. It's Betty-May. I'm sorry I didn't call you earlier. I was out. I was picking it up. (*Dances and makes sounds of pleasure.*) Now, your hair's done, you're going to look fabulous, so don't worry about it. Um um um um ... Look, if you get in and it's early why don't you come over and pick it up okay? Be good to see you. Bye! (*Hangs up. Starts back toward couch. Doorbell CHIMES.*) That was fast. (*Going to door.*) Mary-Margaret, that you? (*Puts chain-lock on door.*) Mary-Margaret? (*Looks through peephole.*) Those fuckin' neighbor kids, goddamn it. (*Retreats from door. BANGING on door.*) Little bastards. Who is it? (*Returns to door.*) I'm not ... (*Opens door to the extent the chain allows, looks around.*) What in the gay hell ...? (*As HE opens the door, a baby begins to CRY. Picks up basket with SQUALLING infant, looks up and down hallway, brings the basket in, paces, places the basket on the sofa, mouths soundlessly to the audience.*) It's a baby! (*Moves basket to top of dresser, finds piece of paper pinned to the Baby blanket.*) It's a note! (*Unfolds it and reads.*) "His name is Dorian. I couldn't take care of him. I hope you can." (*Looks frantically from note to Baby and back.*) Shit! ... Shh! Shh! Kid, you're gonna get me in trouble. We're not allowed to have babies in here because we ... (*Notices donut in his hand.*) A donut! You want a donut, kid? Okay, here you go, here you go. (*Hands donut into basket. BABY tosses donut back out. JERRY retrieves donut from floor and tosses it into garbage.*) Hey look, kid. If you don't want to eat the bloody donut just say so! We're gonna communicate in this house if you're gonna stay here. We're not ... Oh, I'm sorry kid, I'm sorry, I didn't mean to yell, stop crying, no no no no, don't cry, please don't cry, don't cry ... (*Picks up BABY, paces.*) I know, yes, right right, God, yes yes, no no. Come here kid, let me see, let me see baby, let me see ... (*Opens swaddling clothes, looks at BABY's face, makes SOUND of distress.*) Anybody else survive that accident? (*Comforts squalling infant, who quiets down.*) God. Okay okay. Sleepy-sleepy. Sleep sleep sleep, sleep sleep. There you are. Him is my baby now, yah-yo. (*Telephone RINGS, BABY begins crying again.*) Okay, don't cry, don't cry, it's only the phone, we don't even know who's on it ... (*Moves toward phone. Baby's piercing cry hurts his ear. HE puts mewling infant down in basket.*) Shh shh shh shh shh shh shh shh shh ... (*Picks up phone.*) Hello, Yi! Mary-Margaret? Guess what? I came home, and there was a knock on my door and ... yeah, red, just the way it always is, but guess what, guess what? I came home, and there was a knock ... No, I'm not gonna be able to bring it to you. Well yeah, I know I told you I would but I can't, something's come up. I came home, and a knock ... Darling, I do not always do this to you! How can you talk to me like that? You're calling me a ... All right, all right, I can't do it, just send him over. Is he okay? They gave him back his license? Okay, yeah, all right, okay, okay. Yeah. You're gonna come and get me at midnight. Look, I'm not gonna let you punish me like this, for God's sake. You have to come and get me at midnight, you said you would. I can't go out of the house dressed like that anyway. Okay. Who goes on first, you or me? You? I go on last! (*Starts dancing, sings snatch of disco song softly.*) Gloria! Gloria! (*Stops.*) Yes, okay, yeah, goodbye, yes, I love you too. (*Hangs up. Makes series of percussive noises as HE returns to the Baby, reaches into basket, makes sour face, retreats.*) No wonder he's so upset. He's got a big shit in there! (*Grabs huge wad of paper towels and a dishtowel.*) Okay, okay, let's do, let's do. (*Sings.*) Here I come to save the day! (*Makes sounds of flying through the air. Begins to change Baby in basket. Gags. Pulls out old, shit-smeared diaper, displays it to the audience, tosses it out window, grabs more paper towels, wipes bars of window guard with them, drops them out window, returns to Baby, looks at him.*) Well what are you laughing at? Must be Irish. (*Wipes hands on wad of towels, goes back to work on Baby in basket, gags struggles, tosses towels out window, tries to wave away stench, grabs aerosol hair spray, sprays air, sniffs in a satisfied manner, sprays*

A TALE OF TWO CITIES

himself, folds dishtowel into vague triangular diaper shape.) Darling, I don't know. I told them not to make me take wood shop but no, they wouldn't listen. I knew ... (*Approaches Baby with apprehension, plunges in.*) Shit! (*Looks around, grabs hair clasp from wig on table to serve as diaper pin, pins diaper.*) Yes, good baby! Now him is a clean baby. Yes! And a clean baby is a comfy baby. Yes! And a comfy baby is going to take a nap. Yes! 'Cause guess who's making his debut at Sally's tonight, kid? Yeah, you're looking at him. (*Dances. Sings softly.*) Gloria! Gloria! (*Stops.*) Well what are we going to do about you, though? Well darling I just met you. I don't know any babysitters ... What shit! Well why don't you just come with me. Oh, no, don't worry about it. There's lots of fabulous queens. You'll have a ball. (*Grabs hairspray. BABY begins to cry.*) Oh kid, come on! I know this is an upsetting time for you, but I've got to get ready. This is big. I've been waiting a whole month to do this. (*BABY cries even louder.*) Okay okay okay. All right all right all right all right. I'll make a deal with you, okay? One bedtime story, then you've got to take a nap. Yes yes. I know, I know, I know! But that's the deal, kid. (*Taking Baby from basket.*) Tomorrow we'll solve your problems, but tonight's my night. (*Pacing the floor with Baby.*) We'll get you a good psychiatrist tomorrow, we'll talk about it always, talk about , um um um, okay. Once upon a time there were three bears. There was the mama bear,

there was the papa bear, and there was the baby
... You don't like that. All right, don't be scared,
don't be scared, it's only bears, only bears, it
doesn't mean anything. Um. Okay. Rapunzel!
Rapunzel! Let down your golden hair! And this
real hot prince climbs up the hair and ... (*Does
bump with groin. To audience..*) It's a straight
baby. (*Paces.*) Don't worry about it, kid. We can
co-exist. It's a big world. There's room for
everyone. We'll prove it, right in this house,
you'll see. Um. Did you hear the one about Little
Red Riding Hood? She's walking through the
woods, see? And the wolf jumps out from behind
a tree and says, "Little Red Riding Hood? I'm
gonna fuck you right here in the woods!" And
Little Red Riding Hood pulls out her .45 and she
says, "Uh-uh, buddy! You're gonna eat me just
like it says in the book! (*Realizes this isn't
working either, paces frantically.*) It was the best
of times, it was the worst of times. It was the
season of light, it was the season of darkness. We
had everything before us, we had nothing before
us. In short, it was a period just like the pre ...
(*Notices BABY has stopped crying.*) Huh! Just
like the present! Okay, okay. All right, now be a
good boy. Okay. (*Places Baby on couch, sits.*)
Yes yes, lie still for mommy. I have to think now,
I have to think, it's been a long time. (*Thinks.*)
Okay, There's this old Englishman, see, and he's
gonna go to Dover. You know, that's in England.
Well, yes, there's one in Delaware too, but ...
And he's gonna meet this young French girl,

that's it, that's it. And he's gonna take her to Paris and ... It's business, you little pig! (*Stands.*) God that's a cool kid! (*BABY begins to cry again.*) Okay, wait wait wait wait. (*Enacts story.*)

MR. LORRY. Good day, Miss Manette! My name is Mr. Jarvis Lorry, of Tellson's Bank in London. I kiss your hand!

LUCY. (*Curtseying.*) Pray, take a seat, sir. (*Takes frozen food from freezer, places it in microwave.*) I received a letter yesterday from your bank, informing me of some intelligence or discovery.

MR. LORRY. (*Setting timer.*) Well, the word is not material, miss. Either word will do.

LUCY. Respecting a small property of my poor father. Are you quite a stranger to me, sir?

MR. LORRY. I am a man of business. I have a business charge to acquit myself of. (*Stretches out on back of couch.*) In your reception of it, please do not heed me any more than if I were a talking machine. Truly! For I am little else. I will, with your leave, relate to you the story of one of our customers. A French gentleman. A scientific gentleman. A gentleman of great acquirement in Paris. A doctor.

LUCY. But sir! This is my father's story! And I believe the ...

MR. LORRY. So far, Miss Manette, this is the story of your regretted father. But now comes the difference. If ... if Dr. Manette had not died when he did ... My, how you start! (*Getting up, taking up Baby.*) No no, please, please do not be frightened, please, please, please, please. (*Sees Baby's face, makes small sound of distress, covers baby's face again.*) *If* Dr. Manette had not died when he did ... if he had suddenly and silently disappeared ... if he had been swept away ... if it had been difficult to guess to what dreadful place, where no art could trace him ... if he had an enemy who could consign him to the oblivion of prison for any length of time ... if his wife had implored the king, the queen, the court, the clergy, for any news of him (*Returns Baby to basket.*), but all in vain ... Why do you kneel to me miss? For heaven's sake why do you kneel to me?

LUCY. (*Kneeling.*) For the truth. Oh dear good compassionate sir. For the truth!

MR. LORRY. (*After considering.*) You father has been found. He is alive. Yes yes, he has been taken to the house of an old servant in Paris. (*Seating himself and LUCY on couch.*) We are going there. But ... it is a secret service altogether. My credentials can only be understood in one line: *recalled to life!*

(*Thunder. LIGHTS dim and flicker. Baby's basket shakes.*)

LUCY. It would be his ghost? It would not be him! It would be his ghost! Ah ... I'm fainting!

MR. LORRY. Good heaven! Help me! Somebody help me! (*Goes to door. Becomes ...*)

MISS PROSS. (*Screams.*) Now look at you all! Why don't you go and fetch things instead of standing there staring at me? I'm not so much to look at, am I? I'll let you know if you don't fetch me smelling salts and cold water and vinegar quick, I will! Oh, my lady-bird! (*Taking and rubbing her hands.*) Pross is with you now! (*To Mr. Lorry.*) And you, in brown, couldn't you have told her what you had to tell her without frightening her half to death? And you call yourself a banker?

MR. LORRY. Madame ...

MISS PROSS. I am not "Madame." I am Miss Pross, Miss Lucy's companion.

MR. LORRY. I hope ... that she will be all right.

MISS PROSS. No thanks to you in brown if she is!

MR. LORRY. I hope, in that case, you will accompany Miss Manette to Paris.

MISS PROSS. A likely thing. If ever it was intended that I should ever cross salt water, do you suppose Providence would have cast me lot on this island? Oh look at her! With her pretty pale face, and her cold, cold hands!

JERRY. (*Looks around, notices Baby is quiet, gestures to Mr. Lorry to be quiet, looks in basket, sees Baby is sleeping, steps aside, dances and sings in a whisper.*) Gloria! (*Tiptoes to microwave, turns it off, opens door and removes food, burning fingers, takes off plastic wrap, throws it in garbage, gets fork, examines it, wipes it on pants, looks at Baby, smiles, looks at plate, scowls, smiles again, sits on arm of couch, sniffs food, makes ugly face, pretends to be airplane complete with sound effects, scoops forkful of food into mouth, burns himself and makes appropriate noises, chews, satisfied.)* Du jour, Du jour!! *(Kisses fork, sits on dresser, looks in on Baby, gestures to indicate that he can't talk because his mouth is full, chews.)* A large cask of wine had been dropped and broken in the streets, it ... *(Realizes Baby might like food, spears some on fork, offers it to Baby, has difficulty removing his arm from the basket, finally notices fork has been bent, makes appropriate noises, stares in amazement and distress, puts plane down, takes up Baby.)* The accident happened in getting it out of the cart. The cask tumbled out with a run. Its hoops had burst. *(Burps Baby.)* And it lay on the street just outside of the door of the wine shop, shattered like a walnut shell. Here it comes. Okay, baby, let it go, let it go. *(BABY burps hugely. Its face is revealed: old, shrivelled, snot running from its nose. JERRY makes appropriate noises, puts Baby back in basket, dumps food in garbage.)* All the people within reach had suspended their business and the uglin ... ioglness ...*(Pauses to look at Baby.)* ... their idleness ... And ran to the spot to drink the wine. *(Fiddles with bathtub.)* The wine was red, and it stained the ground of the narrow street in the suburb of St. Antoine in Paris. One tall joker, with his head more out of a long squalid bag of a nightcap than in it, scrawled on the wall with his finger, dipped in the muddy wine lees ... (*Grabs ketchup, and scrawls the word "BLOOD" on the tiles of the bathroom wall.*)

MME. DEFARGE. No my Gaspard. The time will come (*Gesturing toward "BLOOD".*) when that wine too will be spilt on the street stones, and the stain of it will run red upon us all. Look at them, grovelling in the street to drink spilled wine. It's not often that many of these miserable beasts know the taste of anything but black bread and death. (*Doorbell rings.*) Strangers!

JERRY. (*Takes up wig, puts white rose in it, hands it through door.*) Here you go. Take this right to him, Ralphie, and don't stop and get drunk on the way. (*Goes to closet. Bell rings.*)

LUCY. Madame Defarge? (*Curtseys.*)

(*JERRY grabs very large needles used for lace work sticks them into crocheted blanket on back of couch.*)

MME. DEFARGE. (*Knitting.*) Oui?
MR. LORRY. Recalled to life!
MME. DEFARGE. (*Knitting.*) Yes. We have a very fine old wine downstairs. I will show it to you. (*Gestures direction with head. Watches them cross room, puts down knitting.*) The stairs are very steep. (*Opens nonexistent trap door.*) It's better to begin slowly. (*Starts down stairs behind couch.*)

LUCY. Is he alone, then?

MME. DEFARGE. Yes, God help him. Who should be with him?

MR. LORRY. Of his own desire?

MME. DEFARGE. Of his own necessity!

MR. LORRY. (*At door to apartment.*) Look! This door is locked!

LUCY. Do you think it necessary to keep my poor father so retired?

MME. DEFARGE. I think it necessary to turn the key. He would be frightened. He would rave. He would tear himself to pieces. He would die. I know not what harm he would come to if the door were left open.

MR. LORRY. Is it possible ...?

MME. DEFARGE. Is it possible? Yes. And a beautiful world we live in when it is possible, and when many other such things are possible and ... not only possible, but done—done, see you! Under that sky there, every day. Long live the devil! Let us go in. (*Does so.*) Good day, monsieur. (*Gestures others to be silent.*) You're working hard, I see?

DR. MANETTE. (*Working at a wig on a block on Jerry's dressing table.*) Yes, I am working

MME. DEFARGE. There are visitors, monsieur. (*To Mr. Lorry.*) Come, monsieur. Tell monsieur the kind of shoe, and the maker's name!

DR. MANETTE. (*Disturbed.*) What ... what was the question? I can't remember what you asked me!

MME. DEFARGE. Tell monsieur the kind of shoe.

DR. MANETTE. (*Displaying wig block.*) It is a lady's shoe. It is a young lady's walking shoe. It ... it is of the present mode. I never saw the mode before. I had a picture of it here, in my head. (*Stabs wig block with rat tail comb groans as if he had stabbed himself.*)

MME. DEFARGE. And the maker's name.

DR. MANETTE. Did you ask me my name?

MME. DEFARGE. Yes, monsieur. I did.

DR. MANETTE. (*Rising, confused and troubled.*) It's ... it's one hundred and five, north tower!

MR. LORRY. No, sir. You are not a shoemaker by trade.

DR. MANETTE. I am not a shoemaker by trade?

MR. LORRY. No, sir. Do you have no recollection of me? I am Mr. Jarvis Lorry, of Tellson's Bank in London.

DR. MANETTE. Yes ... for a moment I ... I've unquestionably seen the face of a man I once knew so well! ... Hush! Let us draw back. Hush! Who are you? (*Threatening them with his comb.*) No! You are ... you're not the jailer's daughter! (*Drops implement.*) How now? Your hair ... your hair? It is the same color as hers! How can that be? When was it? How was it?

LUCY. If ... when I tell you, dearest dear, that your agony is over, and that I've come to take you from it and ... and ... and that ... that ... we go to England to be at rest and at peace ... if I should cause to think of your useful life laid waste

... and of your native France, so wicked to you ... weep for it. Weep for it! (*Kneeling*.) And if, when I shall tell you of my name, and of my father, who is living, and of my poor mother, who is dead, you will learn that I have to kneel to my honored father, and beg him to forgive me, for never having striven all day on his behalf, nor laid awake at night and wept for him, because the love of my poor mother hid his torture from me ... weep for it. Weep for it! (*Wipes tears from eyes*.) Weep for her then, and for me. My friends. All must be arranged for our leaving Paris at once. (*To Mme. Defarge*.) Consider, Madame. Is he fit for the journey?

MME. DEFARGE. Dr. Manette is for all reasons best out of France ... for his sake, and for the sake of all of the secret society of Jacques who helped him. I will hire a carriage. I will post horses here. I can secure the necessary documents. But we must spirit him out of the city. You must leave by the back alley. The city is not safe for him. They will soon discover him missing from his cell, and then they will come looking for him. There is a packet ship for England this afternoon. You must be on it. If you are not, they will find him, and then there will be nothing more that I can do for any of you.

LUCY. Oh my poor father! I hope you care to be recalled to life!

DR. MANETTE. (*Laughing softly but madly, stretching himself across the Baby's basket*.) I can't say that I do, baby.

(*The sound of horses hooves and a carriage.*)

JERRY. With a wild rattle and clatter, and an inhuman abandonment not easy to understand in these times, the carriage dashed through the streets and swept round corners, with women screaming before it, and men clutching each other, and clutching children out of the way ... (*Tumbles over couch.*) At last, swooping round a street corner down by a fountain, one of its wheels came to a sickening jolt. (*Grabs boxes of cereal from a kitchen shelf.*) There was a loud cry from a number of voices (*Grabbing a feather from the bookcase, attaching it to the top of the boxes, making a plumed hat and putting it on.*), and the horses reared and plunged ...

(*The horses stop.*)

GASPARD. (*Screams.*) Ah!
MARQUIS. How now? What has gone wrong?
DRIVER. Pardon, Monsieur le Marquis, it is a child!
MARQUIS. And why does he make that abominable noise? Is it his child?
DRIVER. Pardon, Monsieur le Marquis. It is a pity. Yes.
GASPARD. Dead! Oh no, God! Killed! (*Weeps piteously.*)

MARQUIS. It is extraordinary to me that you people cannot take better care of yourselves and your children. One or the other of you is forever in the way. And how do I know what harm you have done my horses? Go see! (*Annoyed by Gaspard's weeping.*) Oh! (*Reaching into his pocket and tossing out a coin.*) Give him this.

GASPARD. *Dead!*

MME. DEFARGE. Be a brave man, my Gaspard. I know all. I know all! It is better for the little plaything to have died in a moment without pain. Could it have lived an hour as happily?

MARQUIS. You are a philosopher, Madame. How are you called?

MME. DEFARGE. I am Madame Defarge.

MARQUIS. Of what trade?

MME. DEFARGE. (*Rolling the word on her tongue.*) Vendor of wine.

MARQUIS. Well (*tosses out another coin.*) pick up that, philosopher and vendor of wine. But take care how you spend it. (*To his driver.*) Drive on! (*A coin is thrown.*) Hold the horses! Who threw at the carriage? You dogs! I would willingly ride over any of you, and exterminate you from the face of the earth. If I knew which rascal threw at the carriage, and if that brigand were sufficiently near it, I would crush him under its wheels. (*To his driver.*) Drive on!

(*JERRY takes off hat and tosses it into the closet.*)

GASPARD. The Marquis drives fast.

MME. DEFARGE. We'll drive him fast, my good Gaspard. (*Looking into the Baby's basket.*) We'll drive him fast ... to his tomb! You are destined for greater things, my Gaspard, (*Grabs up scissors from kitchen.*) then revenge for the murder of your child! You will light a spark that will kindle all of France! Now go! (*Offering scissors to Gaspard.*) Go to the chateau of Monsieur le Marquis St. Evremonde and kill him, kill him good! The time has begun. Strike terror into the hearts of all who should fear the name of Jacques! Go!

(*GASPARD exits murderously into the closet. Chamber music plays. The MARQUIS emerges from the closet dressed in 18th century coat, goes to the kitchen, pours himself a Coke as if it were wine, sips.*)

MARQUIS. (*To Baby.*) You are ugly. Did you mother feed you with a slingshot? (*BABY pisses on him HE stalks away.*) How now, my dear nephew? What goes forward?

CHARLES. I am leaving for England. You have made the name of Evremonde the most detested in all of France. I can no longer endure your cruelty to the peasants. Do you have no pity for those who suffer?

MARQUIS. There is a sickness these days, which labels itself humanitarianism. It appalls me, Charles, that you actually take this new philosophy of equality seriously. Pah! Pity, my dear boy, is a disease of a particular variety. Tell me, Charles. Do you pity the swine whose flesh you eat?

CHARLES. The peasants are not swine.

MARQUIS. That, my dear boy, is where you and I differ.

CHARLES. Our land is stolen, and I mean to see it returned to the peasants, where it belongs.

MARQUIS. Really, Charles. You may thank your lucky stars that you are related to me. Otherwise, I should have you thrown into the Bastille.

CHARLES. It will not be the first time you have committed such an outrage, uncle.

MARQUIS. I am not at all sure that it would not be the patriotic thing to imprison you ... despite the great personal pain that it might cause me.

CHARLES. I am not afraid of anything that you can do to me, uncle. Goodbye.

MARQUIS. Bon voyage, Mr. Darnay. (*When Charles has gone, becomes aware of a presence, groans.*) Come in, Mr. Barsad.

(*JERRY takes cape off coat rack, tosses around shoulders, hunches over.*)

BARSAD. With pleasure, you excellency.

MARQUIS. My nephew has become an irritant that I wish no longer to contend with. I want him out of the way, quickly and quietly. They tell me that you can accomplish such things.

BARSAD. I can accomplish many things, excellency. For a price.

MARQUIS. Then name your price!

BARSAD. No! I never discuss such things. I leave that to your sense of fairness, to your generosity.

MARQUIS. (*Reaching into his pocket and handing him a large crystal.*) Very well then. He leaves this afternoon. On a packet ship for England.

BARSAD. England is so lovely this time of year. Well how does treason suit you? Ooh— capital Capital.

MARQUIS. And how will you do this?

BARSAD. Well, I will sidle up to him on the boat, sir, and I will slip some incriminating documents into his pocket. Well do not trouble yourself, excellency. Suffice it to say that he will be arrested. He will be tried. And he will be convicted. I am oh so terribly good at my work. And now I must be off if I am to catch that ship this afternoon. It's a pity Mr. Darnay will not get to enjoy England. It is so lovely this time of year.

JERRY. (*After hanging up cape, looking at Baby, and counting ten silently to himself.*) Darling, stay awake, you're gonna learn something, 'cause I'm going to get this to ... (*Turns on radio.*)

RADIO. (*Not Jerry.*) You give us twenty-two minutes, we'll give you the world. And now, live from London, our British correspondent, Minnie Beamish.

CORRESPONDENT. (*Not Jerry*.) Charles Darnay had yesterday pleaded "Not Guilty" to an indictment denouncing him (with infinite jingle and jangle) for that he was a false traitor to our serene, illustrious, excellent, and so forth, prince, Our Lord the King, by reason of his having, on divers occasion, and by divers means and ways, assisted Lewis, the French King, in his wars against our said serene, illustrious, excellent, and so forth, that was to say by coming and going, between the dominions of our said serene illustrious, excellent, and so forth, and those of the said Lewis, and wickedly, falsely, traitorously, and otherwise evil-adverbiously, revealing to the said French Lewis what forces our said serene, illustrious, excellent, and so forth, had in preparation to send to Canada and North America. The court was all bestrewn with herbs and sprinkled with vinegar as a precaution against jail air and jail fever.

(*During the news broadcast, JERRY runs water in the bathtub and strips down to socks and underpants, tossing the rest of his clothes into the closet. Harpsichord music follows the news report, and after listening a while, JERRY turns off the radio.*)

JERRY. I don't like that. (*HE tests the water's temperature, looks out window to see if anyone is looking, returns to the tub, gasps.*) You! Get out! I don't want you in my apartment. Get out! You have no right to be here! (*Gasps, covers his nakedness, caresses himself with his arms as if they belonged to someone else.*) No! What are you doing? No, don't make me do it again, please, please! No, please, please!

(*JERRY suggests striptease music, performs striptease, strips off layered socks, pulls down front of underwear and flashes at the window, removes wig revealing his baldness, strips off and sniffs underpants, hops into tub, emits shriek of pain, splashes his face and hair with water, turns off the taps, transforms into Sidney Carton.*)

SIDNEY. Strange chance that throws you and me together, Mr. Darnay. Must seem strange to you, standing alone at night on the street stones with your counterpart.

CHARLES. I hardly seem to belong to this world again, Mr. Carton.

SIDNEY. I don't wonder at it. Not very long since you were pretty far advanced on your way to another. You speak rather faintly.

CHARLES. Yes, Mr. Carton. I begin to think that I am faint.

SIDNEY. Then why the devil don't you dine, hmm? I dined myself while those numbskulls were deliberating whether you should belong to this world or some other. Come along, my friend. I'll take you to the nearest tavern to dine at.

JERRY. (*Splashes face and hair with water, grabs and shakes up aerosol can of shaving cream, lowers it into the tub, seems to masturbate, raises a handful of shaving cream, looks around anxiously.*) Where's my bloody mirror? God! Why isn't anything ever where I put it? Why doesn't anything ever ... (*Mutters imprecations silently, calms down, smiles, retrieves aerosol can from water, startles himself with reflection in bottom of can, realizes it can be his mirror, uses it to lather his face, takes razor in hand.*)

SIDNEY. Tell me my dear Darnay, do you begin to feel that you belong to this terrestrial scheme again? As for me, the greatest desire I have is to forget that I belong to it. It has no good in it for me (*Referring to aerosol can.*), except wine like this, of course. Nor I for it. No. I see we are not much alike in that particular. I begin to think that we are not much alike in any particular, you and I. (*Belches, uses bottom of can as mirror, shaves.*) Now that you have dined, my dear Darnay. Why don't you call a health? Why don't you raise a toast?

CHARLES. A health? A toast?

SIDNEY. Come now, Darnay. It's on the tip of your tongue. It ought to be. I swear it's there.

CHARLES. Very well. Miss Manette, then.

SIDNEY. Miss Manette, then. (*Cuts himself.*) Ah! There's a fair young lady to be pitied for and wept by for. (*Resumes shaving shakily.*) Tell me my dear Darnay, was it worth being tried for your

A TALE OF TWO CITIES 29

life to be the object of such sympathy and compassion?

CHARLES. My dear Mr. Carton, do I detect a note of jealousy?

(SIDNEY startled, splashing himself with water, as if throwing a drink in Charles' face.)

CHARLES. Pray forgive me, sir. I was rude. When did it strike you that you and I looked enough alike to create a sufficient doubt in the minds of the jury, thereby gaining my acquittal? I am very grateful to you for all your assistance.

SIDNEY. I neither want your thanks nor merit any. It was nothing in the first place, and I don't know why I did it in the second. Do you think that I particularly like you?

CHARLES. You act as if you do, but I don't think you do.

SIDNEY. *I* don't think I do. I begin to have a very good opinion of your understanding.

(BABY rises from basket, shakes forward and back. JERRY falls back into tub, as if being drowned. BABY drops back into basket.)

JERRY. (*Emerging from water, spluttering and gasping, grabbing towel, covering and drying himself.*) What the fuck...?

CHARLES. Then there's nothing to prevent me from calling for the reckoning, and our parting without any ill blood on either side.

SIDNEY. (*Drunkenly stumbling out of tub.*) Tell me, my dear Darnay, do you go for the whole reckoning?

CHARLES. Yes, Mr. Carton, I do. The whole reckoning.

SIDNEY. Well in that case ... (*Taking aerosol can with him toward closet, as if it were a bottle of spirits.*) Waiter! Bring me another pint of this wine! And come and wake me at ten! (*Returning with a stagger toward the tub.*) May I ask you a question, Darnay? Do you think that I am drunk?

CHARLES. I think you have been drinking.

SIDNEY. You know I have been drinking. I'll tell you why. (*Falling partway into the tub, leaving can there.*) I am a disappointed drudge, Mr. Darnay. I care for no man on earth, and no man on earth cares for me.

CHARLES. Much to be regretted. You might have used your talents better.

SIDNEY. (*Staggered.*) Maybe yes, Mr. Darnay, and maybe no. Don't let your sober face elate you, Darnay. You don't know where it's going to take you now, do you? (*Sitting on arm of couch, waving.*) Goodnight. (*Falls onto and passes out on couch.*)

(*Alarm clock sounds. JERRY hastens to shut it off.*)

JERRY. Okay, all right, I can hear you. For God's sake shut up! (*Opens closet, tosses in towel, pulls out and dons pajama pants.*)

DR. MANETTE. (*Startled, caught off-guard.*) Me dear Mr. Darnay! Do come in. Yes, Mr. Carton was here yesterday. He warned us that you were past due. Miss Manette? Miss Manette isn't home. (*Puts on slippers.*) She has gone out on some household errands or other ... She will return shortly. I think she will be delighted to see you.

CHARLES. Dr. Manette, I knew that Miss Manette was away from home. I took the opportunity of her being out to beg to speak to you. I love your daughter dearly, devotedly, disinterestedly. You have loved yourself, please let your past love speak for me now.

DR. MANETTE. (*Climbing on couch and dangling from ceiling.*) Not that! Let that be! Do not recall that to my mind! Not that! Pray do not ask it of me. What do you want from me?

CHARLES. A promise.

DR. MANETTE. Eh what, what's that?

CHARLES. If I were to ask Miss Manette ... Oh Doctor, do be careful up there, please, for God's sake! If I were to ask Miss Manette to be my wife, and she agreed, that you would do nothing to influence her against me.

DR. MANETTE. (*Balancing precariously on top of couch.*) I give you my word. Without any reservation. (*Sitting on couch, rising with a shout, having been stabbed in the butt by a knitting needle.*)

CHARLES. Your confidence in me ought to be returned with full confidence on my part. My present name is not my own. I wish to tell you what it is, and why I am in England. (*Sitting on couch.*) I have just learned something which distresses me very deeply. It is a bitter irony ... that the man who caused you such dreadful injustice should be my ... blood relation. I am an Evremonde. (*Thunder and lightning. Arm with knife rises from basket momentarily. JERRY rises, walks across top of couch, descends.*) But I love you and yours! I would give my life for you or for Lu ...

DR. MANETTE. (*Retreating into corner.*) Evremonde? No! Get away from my coach. Get away! Who are you? No! No! You will pay for your crimes! If you do not pay here, you will pay in the eyes of God! No, please! Where are you taking me? Please, no! (*Takes bottle of tranquilizers from kitchen shelf, drinks.*) No, please, I have a wife! No, not the Bastille! Please! My wife ... will be alone! My child! Oh oh oh oh God, okay, okay, it's over now, it's over ... (*Calming down.*) Charles. It took a great deal of courage for you to come to me with this information. I am very grateful to you. No, I will not hold it against you. I ... I am too old. Ah ... you ... you must not tell Lucy, please. There is no telling how she would react. She has not had the time that I have had ... I insist that you do not tell her. There is no telling how she would re ... If you defy me ... Leave my home at once! Please, Lucy will return shortly. She must not find us alone together!

JERRY. (*Opening closet door.*) Oh God, this closet is alive. (*Comes out with billowing white cap. Straps a pannier skirt of bird cages and hat boxes around his waist. Takes up a paper-wrapped bunch of flowers, closes closet door.*)

LUCY. My dear Mr. Carton! I fear that you are not well.

SIDNEY. The life I lead, Miss Manette, is not conducive to health.

LUCY. (*Replacing old flowers in bookcase with fresh ones.*) It's a pity that you live no better life.

SIDNEY. God knows it is a shame.

LUCY. Then why not change it, sir?

SIDNEY. I shall never be better than what I am. I shall only sink lower, and be worse. (*Weeping sounds.*)

LUCY. My dear.

SIDNEY. Pray forgive me, Miss Manette. I break down before the knowledge of what I am about to say to you. Will you hear me?

LUCY. If it would do you any good, sir. If it would make you happier, then it would make me very glad.

SIDNEY. God bless you, Miss Manette, for your sweet compassion.

(*LUCY curtseys.*)

SIDNEY. Do not be afraid to hear me. Do not shrink from anything I say to you. I am like one who died young. All my life might have been ...

LUCY. No, sir. I feel that the greater part of it might yet be.

SIDNEY. (*Taking off cap, leaving it on couch.*) Though in my wretched heart I know better, I shall never forget you said so. I know you can have no tenderness for me. I ask for none. I am even grateful that it cannot be. My one supplication in all is this, and then I will relieve you of a visitor with whom you have nothing in unison, and between whom there is an impassable space. It is useless to say, but it rises from my soul. I would embrace any sacrifice for you, Miss Manette, or for those dear to you. Know you, now and then, that there is a man who would give his life to keep a life you love beside you. Farewell, Miss Manette.

LUCY. (*Taking up cap, crossing to and opening closet door, tossing cap in, waving.*) God bless you, Sidney. (*Taking off skirt, tossing that in, closing closet door and leaning back against it.*) God bless you.

MME. DEFARGE. (*Crossing to basket.*) What? (*Taking up Baby.*) What did Jacques of the police tell you? (*Holding Baby to ear.*) There's a new spy commissioned to our quarter. What is his name? (*BABY whispers.*) He's an Englishman? So much the better. How is he called? (*BABY whispers.*) Hah! John Barsad! Tell me, my little one, is it necessary to register him? (*BABY nods yes. MME. DEFARGE returns him to his basket.*) Then I will register him tomorrow.

(*Bell rings. JERRY dons cloak.*)

BARSAD. Good day, Madame. Have the goodness to give me a glass of old cognac, and a glass of fresh water.

(*SHE does. HE drinks, shrieks, and gasps.*)

BARSAD. It's a marvelous cognac, this. You knit well, Madame.
MME. DEFARGE. (*Miming work with a skein of wool.*) I am accustomed to it.
BARSAD. And what do you make?
MME. DEFARGE. Many things.
BARSAD. For instance?
MME. DEFARGE. For instance ... shrouds.
BARSAD. John Barsad at your service.
MME. DEFARGE. (*Working the thread.*) How many "d's" in Barsad?
BARSAD. Madame?
MME. DEFARGE. Monsieur?

(*THEY glance back and forth at each other.*)

BARSAD. Have you a husband, Madame?
MME. DEFARGE. Yes.
BARSAD. His name is Jacques?
MME. DEFARGE. You are mistaken, sir. My husband's name is Ernest.
BARSAD. Oh, yes indeed, Ernest. The pleasure of conversing with you, Madame, recalls to me that I've had the honor of cherishing some

very interesting associations with your name. I have known a Dr. Manette and his daughter in England. You hear much about them?

MME. DEFARGE. No. In effect, we never hear about them. They have gradually taken their own road in life and we ours. We have held no correspondence.

BARSAD. So you do not know then?

(THEY glance back and forth at each other.)

BARSAD. Miss Manette is going to be married.

MME. DEFARGE. Going? She's pretty enough to have been married long ago. Pfft! You English are very cold, it seems to me.

BARSAD. *(Gasping.)* You can tell that I am English?

MME. DEFARGE. I perceive your tongue is, and what the tongue is I suppose the man is.

BARSAD. Perfectly so. But Miss Manette is going to be married, and not to an Englishman, but to one who like herself is French by birth. Hmm. It's a bad business, this, of Gaspard's execution. It was cruel. It was cruel.

MME. DEFARGE. If people use knives for such purposes, then they must pay for it. Gaspard knew what price his luxury was. He has paid that price.

BARSAD. It's a curious thing, though, that Miss Manette is going to marry the nephew of the late Monsieur le Marquis St. Evremonde, the one for whom Gaspard was exalted to that height of so many feet. (*Mimes a hanging, and a broken neck, makes appropriate noises.*) In other words, the present Marquis. He lives in England now. No-o-o-o, he is no Marquis there! His name is Charles Darnay. Darnay is the name of his mother's family. Yes. It has rather an aristocratic ring to it, wouldn't you say, Madame? I must be off. A pleasant day to you, Madame. And a pleasant day to your husband Ja ... Ernest.

(*Bell rings. JERRY hangs up cloak.*)

MME. DEFARGE. (*To Baby.*) Can it be true what he has said about Mademoiselle Manette? As he has said it, it is probably false. (*To herself.*) Yes, but it may be true. Well if it is true, and it does happen while I live to see the triumph, I hope destiny will keep her husband out of France. Long live the devil! (*To Baby.*) The husband's destiny will take him where he is to go. It will lead him to the end that is to end him. That is all I know. For it would be easier for the weakest coward that lives to eradicate himself from the face of the earth than for any man to erase his name or crimes from the knitted register of Madame Defarge! (*Raising blanket that serves as register.*) Citizens! Friends! Hear me! The time is now! The Bastille!

JERRY. (*Removing cushions from couch, pulling out bed.*) With a roar that sounded as if all the breath in France had been shaped into that detested word, the living sea rose, and overflowed the city to that point. (*Revealing painting of the storming of the bastille on bed's underside, waving small French flag found within.*) Alarm bells ringing, drums beating, the living sea, raging and thundering against its new beach, the battle had begun!

MME. DEFARGE. (*Stripping the bed and remaking it with clean sheets.*) Work, comrades all! Work! Work! Jacques one! Jacques two! Jacques one thousand! Jacques five and twenty thousand! Work! Work, comrades all! Work! Work in the name of the angels—or the devils, as you prefer it! Work! You women wait! You can kill as well as the men when this detested place is taken. Citizens! The Bastille! Storm the Bastille! (*Folds up bed, replaces cushions.*) Kill your enemies! Off with their heads! Let none escape! (*Draping himself in sheet.*) The Bastille is fallen! (*Tossing old sheet into closet.*) Long live the Republic! (*Seizing guard by the throat.*) You! Take me to the north tower! Quick!

GUARD. There's no one there, Madame!

MME. DEFARGE. What's the meaning of one hundred and five north tower? Quick!

GUARD. The meaning, Madame?

MME. DEFARGE. Is it a captive, or does it mean a place of captivity? (*Grabbing a knife from the kitchen, lashing out with it.*) Or does it mean that I shall strike you dead on the spot?

GUARD. It's a cell, Madame!

MME. DEFARGE. Take me there, quick!

GUARD. Follow me!

MME. DEFARGE. Run that light along this wall that I may see. Quickly! (*Looks under tub, under bed, out window, into kitchen corner.*) Stop! Look, Jacques! "A.M." So! Here wrote the poor physician! What's that in your hand? A crowbar! Give it to me! (*Takes broom.*) Hold the light higher that I may see. Hold it higher! (*Attacks wall with broom, makes hole, reaches in, gets hand caught in rat trap, screams, takes it off, emerges with piece of paper, reads.*) I have found it! Dr. Manette's letter! I have found it! (*Nears Baby's basket. BABY attempts but fails to snatch letter away.*) Yes, this is it. Ahh! (*Picks up phone.*) Hello, yes. I would like to send a telegram to England. Mr. Charles Darnay, care of Tellson's Bank in London. Yes yes, I will wait, thank you. (*Referring to Guard.*) Lock him in, and burn the place to the ground. (*Into telephone.*) Hello, yes. Come quick. Stop. My life is in danger. Stop. I am in the hands of the Republicans. Stop. Only your testimony can save me now. Stop. Signed, ah, Gabelle. Monsieur Gabelle, yes. Gabelle, Gabelle. Gabelle. Elle elle elle. Yes. Ah oui, madame, ah oui, oui. (*Hangs up phone.*) Merci, monsieur. (*Looks at letter, places it on dressing table, crosses to kitchen, raises a can of Coke.*) To the Republic! (*Drinks.*)

JERRY. (*Taking black corset from closet and donning it.*) A very few leagues of his French journey were accomplished when Charles Darnay perceived that for him, along these French country roads, there was no hope of return, unless he should have been declared a good citizen of Paris. Whatever might befall him now, he must go on to his journey's end. (*Removes slippers and bloomers.*)

REPUBLICAN OFFICER. Halt! Advance to be recognized! Your papers!

CHARLES. (*Taking pantyhose from dressing table drawer and donning them.*) Here they are! Here they are!

REPUBLICAN OFFICER. Ah! Emigrant! I'm going to send you to Paris, under an escort!

CHARLES. Well, I desire nothing more than to go to Paris. But I, I would dispense with the escort.

REPUBLICAN OFFICER. Silence! Peace, aristocrat! You are an aristocrat. You are an emigrant. Well you must go to Paris, you must have an escort, and you must pay for it.

CHARLES. I have no choice then ...

REPUBLICAN OFFICER. (*Spits at him.*) You are a curséd aristocrat, and a curséd emigrant. Your useless life, Evremonde, has been forfeit to the Republic. You have been judged and condemned as a traitor.

CHARLES. My friends, you deceive yourselves, or you are deceived. I am not a traitor!

REPUBLICAN OFFICER. You lie, Evremonde! You have been condemned to the prison of La Force.

CHARLES. Under what law? For what offense?

REPUBLICAN OFFICER. There are new laws, Evremonde. And new offenses since you were here.

CHARLES. I entreat you to observe that I have come here voluntarily, in response to a written appeal from a fellow countryman, which lies before you. (*Putting on panties.*) I demand no more than the opportunity to do so without delay. Is that not my right?

REPUBLICAN OFFICER. Emigrants have no rights, Evremonde! Sit down!

(*Forcing Charles onto dressing table chair. CHARLES puts on silver high heels.*)

REPUBLICAN OFFICER. Keep silent! Or you may not make it to Paris.

(*CHARLES straightens hose.*)

REPUBLICAN OFFICER. Jailor! Jailor! The emigrant Evremonde, in secret, too.

JAILOR. (*Grabbing paper towels from kitchen, wiping himself.*) Oh, what the devil! Not another one? As if we were not already full to bursting. Well where do you think that I am going to put them, for heaven's sake? As if ... Pardon, monsieur. Follow me, Evremonde. (*Advances to dressing table.*) In secret, too. Tch tch tch tch tch tch tch! What a pity.

CHARLES. (*Sitting.*) I do not understand the meaning of the term, "in secret."

JAILOR. (*Applying base to face.*) Well, many members of your society have been kept in secret ... for a little while. (*Indicates the slicing of a throat, with appropriate sound effect, then carefully smoothes base.*) Here is your cell.

CHARLES. Tell me, why am I confined alone?

JAILOR. How should I know?

CHARLES. Can I buy ink and pen and paper?

JAILOR. Such are not my orders. (*Powdering down.*) You will be visited, and then you can ask. In the meantime, you can buy your food ... and nothing more.

CHARLES. Oh ... now I am left as if I were dead. (*Gasping.*) And here in these crawling creatures is the first condition of the body after death.

MR. LORRY. (*Donning floor-length dressing coat.*) I pray God that no one near and dear to me is in this dreadful city tonight. God. (*To Baby.*) What's the matter now, my little one, and what is upsetting you now, for heaven's sake. If it isn't one thing it's an ... Are you worried about me? Well let me tell you, little one, I am here in Paris taking care of their money. They're not likely to harm the banker. No one is going to harm the man who's taking care of their money. So let me tell ... (*Reaching into the basket, being bitten.*) Ow ...! May God have mercy on all those who are in danger. Dr. Manette! Lucy! What are you doing here in Paris? I warned you not to follow me!

LUCY. Oh my dear friend, my husband ...
MR. LORRY. Charles? What about Charles?
LUCY. He's here.
MR. LORRY. What?
LUCY. Yes.
MR. LORRY. Where?

LUCY. Here! In Paris! An errand of generosity brought him here unknown to us. He has been stopped at the barrier. They have sent him to prison! I will go to Madame Defarge.

MR. LORRY. No, my dear! She is a dangerous woman!

LUCY. I will go to Madame Defarge. I'm not afraid of her. I will beg her for mercy. She has helped me before (*Bell rings*.) Madame Defarge. There is no need for the white rose, Madame, you know who I am. You will be good to my poor husband. You will do nothing to harm him. You will help me to see him if you can!

MME. DEFARGE. Your husband is not my problem here madame. It is the daughter of your father who is my problem here.

LUCY. Then for my sake, be merciful to my poor husband. For my child's sake. (*Placing a puppet child on her hand*.) She will put out her hands, and she will beg you to have mercy. We are more afraid of you than we are of these times.

MME. DEFARGE. Is this the child?

CHILD. Yes, Madame. I am the poor prisoner's darling daughter and only child.

MME. DEFARGE. (*Grabbing puppet from hand.*) I have seen enough. (*Dropping puppet into water of the tub.*)

LUCY. (*On her knees.*) Madame, I implore you to have pity on me, and not to exercise any power that you possess against my husband, but to use it on his behalf. Oh sister-woman, please! Think of me as a wife and a mother!

MME. DEFARGE. The wives and mothers we've been known to see, since we were as little as that child and much less, have not been greatly considered. We have seen their husbands and their fathers laid in prison and kept from them often enough. We have seen our sister-women suffer, in themselves and in their children, nakedness, hunger, thirst, misery, sickness, oppression, and neglect of all kinds. We have borne this a long time. Judge you! Is it likely that the troubles of one wife and mother would mean much to us now?

LUCY. (*Slapped down my Mme. Defarge.*) No. I am not thankless. I hope. But that dreadful woman seems to cast a shadow over all my hope. (*Weeps.*)

(*JERRY dons three-cornered hat, rings bell.*)

REPUBLICAN PROSECUTOR. Bring in the next prisoner! Ahh! (*Grabs groin suggestively.*) And what is your profession?

SEAMSTRESS. I am a seamstress, citizen.

REPUBLICAN PROSECUTOR. You are accused of consorting openly with one Pierre Cole, who spoke slightingly of the revolution.

SEAMSTRESS. Oh no! He is a friend of mine, citizen. We were raised together in the country.

REPUBLICAN PROSECUTOR. You should choose your friends more wisely, citizeness seamstress. Death within forty-eight hours.

(*SEAMSTRESS gasps.*)

REPUBLICAN PROSECUTOR. Pah! (*Dismisses her with a gesture, rings bell.*) Bring in the next prisoner! Ah! (*Curtseying.*) Monsieur le Marquis St. Evremonde. Also known as Charles Darnay. (*Snickers derisively.*) You are accused, Evremonde, under a decree which forbids the return of all aristocratic emigrants under the penalty of death.

CHARLES. (*Removing hat.*) I submit that I am not an emigrant in that sense of the word. I relinquished my title before the revolution began. I wished to live by my own industry in England, rather than off the already overladened population of France. Dr. Manette will speak for me!

REPUBLICAN PROSECUTOR. Speak, Dr. Manette!

DR. MANETTE. Citizens! Friends! You all know of my long sufferings! And how I was aided by my good friends, the Defarge ... (*Startled by seeing Mme. Defarge.*) I have known Charles Darnay well. In the last few years we have become very close friends. I know where his sympathies lie. They are with you, the people where they have always been! No! He is a true friend of the Republic! What better proof can I give, but that when he asked for my only daughter's hand in marriage, I gave it to him gladly! For eighteen years, I suffered unspeakable tortures in the Bastille. (*Pleading with various wig blocks.*) Could I give my only daughter's hand to a man whose sympathies lie with those who tortured me? (*Making one wig block gesture "No."*) There is very little left for me in this life, citizens. Only the happiness of my daughter, which is now in the hands of the prisoner. I have suffered much from my enemies. But from you, my friends, to whom I owe my liberty, let me ask one final blessing, please! Let me live out the rest of my life in peace! Oh, thank you! Thank you forever! Thank you!

MME. DEFARGE. (*Removing coat.*) Stop!

COURT OFFICER. (*Ringing bell.*) Madame Defarge! You are out of order! Stop! Madame Defarge! You're out of order! Madame De ...!

MME. DEFARGE. I defy your bell! I accuse this man, Evremonde, one of a family of tyrants, who used their privileges for the oppression of the people.

PROSECUTOR. Your witness?

MME. DEFARGE. There are three. Ernest Defarge. (*Indicating self.*) Thérèse Defarge. And ... Dr. Manette!

DR. MANETTE. No! It's a lie! Who dares to say that I denounce this man?

MME. DEFARGE. I do! And you denounce him in words that cannot be taken back.

DR. MANETTE. No! No! I make no accusation!

MME. DEFARGE. How can you say that, Doctor? (*Taking letter from table.*) It is here in black and white. Let me read it for you. Look! (*Reads.*) For all that Evremondes have made me suffer, for all that they have made the people suffer, I, Dr. Alexander Manette (*Points finger at Dr. Manette.*), do, on this last night of the year, and in my unspeakable agony, denounce the family of Evremonde, them and their descendants, to the last of their race! (*Holds letter aloft for all to see.*) This letter was written in prison by Dr. Manette, in scrapings of soot and charcoal mixed with his own blood. Dr. Manette has told you that he spent eighteen years in solitary confinement in the Bastille. Well! This letter tells you why! It tells how, as a young doctor, he was summoned to the bedside of a dying girl. Dying! Because she had been outraged by the Evremondes. It tells of a young boy who was cut down because he dared to come to the defense of his sister. It describes the agony of those two innocent young people. That boy is dead. That girl is dead! All that peasant family but one is dead, through the cruelty and oppression of the Evremondes. All but one— a sister. She was hidden from them, and she lives! She is alive today! (*Standing on the couch.*)

I am that sister! And I demand the life of the last of the Evremondes! I demand it! Citizens! Vote! (*Voices of citizens condemn Charles Darnay.*) How can you stand there snivelling, Doctor? How can you defend the sons of monsters? (*Flings letter in his face.*) Save him now, Doctor ... if you can! Go to the people! Go! I think they will not hear you.

LUCY. Charles! Charles!

CHARLES. Farewell my dearest darling of my heart. We will meet again, where the weary are at rest!

LUCY. No no no no no!

CHARLES. Do not fear for me my darling. I can bear it.

LUCY. (*Retrieving puppet from waters of the tub.*) A parting blessing on our child.

CHARLES. I kiss her. I say farewell to her.

LUCY. (*As Charles is dragged away.*) No. No! One moment! My husband! (*Falling back on couch.*) No! We will not be separated long! For this will break my heart by and by. (*To puppet.*) But I will do my duty while I can. And when I can no longer, I know that God will raise up friends for you, as he did for me. (*Faints.*)

CHILD. Oh Carton, Carton, now that you have come, I know that you will do something to help mama, to save papa. Oh, look at her Carton! How can you who love her bear to see her suffer so?

SIDNEY. (*To puppet.*) Shhh! (*Stuffs her beneath the cushions.*) Miss Pross. Mr. Lorry. (*Donning coat.*) I've come as quickly as I can.

Something I wish to say to you. Sit down ... Do not ask me why I make the stipulations I am about to make, or exact the promise that I am about to exact. I have a reason for it. A good one.

MR. LORRY. No doubt you do, sir.

SIDNEY. I know that I can get in to see Charles Darnay once.

MR. LORRY. What earthly good would it do if you did see him?

SIDNEY. This paper enables me to pass out of the city at any time. You see? Sidney Carton, Englishman. Keep this for me, Mr. Lorry. And here is a similar certificate, which enables Dr. Manette, his daughter, and her child, to pass out of the city and beyond the barrier. Now they are good until they are recalled, and I have reason to believe that they will be recalled soon.

MISS PROSS. Are they in danger?

SIDNEY. Yes, Pross. The are in grave danger. Danger of denunciation from Madame Defarge.

MISS PROSS. Ah!

SIDNEY. You know it is a capital crime to mourn for or to sympathize with any victim of the guillotine. Dr. Manette and his daughter would unquestionably be guilty of that crime. Now listen to me, both of you, and do exactly as I tell you. Do not stray from this one bit, as more depends upon this than you dare know or hope. Early tomorrow morning, you must have horses ready so that they are in starting trim for England before noon. Tonight, you must tell Lucy what you know of the dangers as involving her father and her child. Dwell upon that, as she would lay her own head down beside that of her husband's cheerfully. Press upon her the necessity of leaving Paris with them and you at that time. Quietly and steadily, have all the arrangements made in the courtyard here, even to the taking of your own seat in the carriage. When I come, you must take me in and drive away.

MR. LORRY. I understand that I am to wait for you under all circumstances?

SIDNEY. Wait for nothing but to have my seat occupied. And then for England. Now, goodbye. (*HE leaves and waits upon the edge of the bathtub.*) Mr. Barsad! That you? Can I buy you a drink?

BARSAD. Why?

SIDNEY. Because I have a proposal that I wish to make, for our mutual satisfaction. (*Grabbing him by the back of the lapel.*)

BARSAD. What is it? What do you want?

(*CARTON forces his head into the tub.*)

BARSAD. No! No! I'll hear you! I'll hear you!

SIDNEY. Mr. Barsad. I want an interview. With Charles Darnay. In La Force prison.

BARSAD. No, sir! It's unpossible! It's absolutely unpossible!

SIDNEY. Mr. Barsad ... emissary of the Republican Committee ... now turnkey, now in prison ... always spy and secret informant ... represents himself to his new employers under a false name. Yes. That's a good card. Mr. Barsad ... now in the employ of the French Republican government ... is formerly in the employ of the English aristocratic government, enemy of France and freedom. Yes. That is an excellent card. Inference clear as day in this region of suspicion, is that Mr. Barsad is still in the employ of the English aristocratic government, and is a spy of Pitt, the treacherous foe of the Republic. Now that is a card not to be beaten. Now then, my good Barsad. What do you think of my hand?

BARSAD. I don't understand your play!

SIDNEY. I play my ace. Denunciation of Mr. Barsad to the nearest section committee.

BARSAD. I don't believe you, sir.

SIDNEY. I play my ace, without any scruples in a very few moments. You may depend upon it.

BARSAD. Who am I to doubt you, sir? Follow me.

SIDNEY. (*Removing and hanging up coat.*) Wait here, Barsad, I will go in alone.

CHARLES. (*Seated at the dressing table.*) So, this is the hour of my death. (*Crosses himself.*) Carton, you!

SIDNEY. My dear Mr. Darnay. Of all people on earth, I am the last person you expected to see here tonight.

CHARLES. You're not a prisoner?

SIDNEY. No-o-o-o. I am accidentally in possession of a great power over one of your attendants here. And in virtue of it you see me standing before you. I come from her, dear

Darnay. (*Applying eye shadow from compact.*) Your wife. I bring a message to you.

CHARLES. What is it?

SIDNEY. (*Closing compact.*) You have no time to ask me what it means or why I bring it. I have no time to tell you. You simply must comply with me at once.

CHARLES. Sir!

SIDNEY. Change those boot you wear for these of mine. (*Pulling red high-heeled shoes from beneath table.*)

CHARLES. There can be no escaping from this place. It is madness. You will be caught. You will be killed with me.

SIDNEY. When I tell you to walk through that door, then you tell me it is madness, and then you stay here. In the meantime, sir, do what I tell you. Quickly, quickly!

(*CHARLES changes shoes.*)

SIDNEY. Now sir, change that cravat you wear for this of mine, and that coat you wear for this of mine, and while you do that, let me take the ribbon from your hair and shake it out like this of mine. Now sir, steady yourself. Take up that pencil and write what I tell you.

CHARLES. (*Taking up eyebrow pencil.*) To whom should I address it?

SIDNEY. To no one. Now write. (*Applying pencil.*) "When you receive this, you will recollect the words that passed between us. I know you will remember them. It is not in your nature to forget them." But have you written "forget them?"

CHARLES. Yes, sir.

SIDNEY. Well do not dawdle, my good man. Write on. Write on.

CHARLES. What is that in your hand? Is that a weapon?

SIDNEY. No sir. I am not armed.

CHARLES. What is that in your hand?

SIDNEY. You will know presently. Now write! "I am thankful that the time has come when I can carry out the promise that I made to you. That I do so ... there is no cause for regret, or grief."

JERRY. (*Smudges makeup.*) Shit! Damn it!

CHARLES. (*Opening and sniffing cold cream.*) What is that vapor?

SIDNEY. Vapor? (*Sniffs.*) I am conscious of nothing.

CHARLES. (*Correcting smudge.*) I tell you something crossed me!

SIDNEY. Well I tell you that I am conscious of nothing. And as I am conscious of nothing there can be nothing. Now sir, quickly, take up that pencil and finish writing what I dictate. There is precious little time. Quickly. Quickly! (*Continues making up.*) "If it had been otherwise, I should have all the more to be answerable for." (*Taking a tissue in hand.*) "If it had been other ..."

(*Presses tissue over Charles' nose and mouth. A struggle ensues. CHARLES succumbs, passes out. JERRY blows tissue into the air.*)

SIDNEY. Barsad! Come quick! Take him to the coach!
BARSAD. But Mr. Carton!
SIDNEY. Do not argue with me, Barsad. There is no time. (*Stamps his feet on the ground to simulate sound of running.*) They've gotten clear. Ah! They've gotten clear! (*Laughs.*) Ah, they've gotten clear! (*Applies rouge.*)
PRISON GUARD. Evremonde! The time has come! Follow me!

(*HE does.*)

MME. DEFARGE. (*Looking at Baby.*) I have the race of Evremonde in my register, doomed for destruction and extermination. The wife must follow the husband. The child must follow the father! (*Clutching basket.*) Yes, she'll be at home now. She'll be awaiting the moment of his death. She will be mourning and grieving. She'll be in a state of mind to impeach the justice of the Republic. She will be full of sympathy for its enemies. I will go to her. Take you my knitting. (*Places knitting in basket.*) And keep it for me in my usual seat by the guillotine. Go there straight. There will be a greater concourse there than usual today.

MISS PROSS. (*Pulls skirt of dressing table. Dons it.*) Oh my dear Mr. Cruncher! What do you think? What do you think of another carriage leaving from this courtyard this afternoon? And another carriage having already gone from there this morning. Don't you think that that would awaken suspicion? Oh, I am so full of fear and hope for my little ones that I am not capable of forming any plan. Are you capable of forming any plan, Mr. Cruncher? Oh, for gracious sake, Mr. Cruncher, let us think! (*Pacing.*) If you were to go before, and you were to stop the vehicle and the horses from coming here, and you were to take me in somewhere, wouldn't that be best Mr. Cruncher? Yes? Then where would you take me in? By the cathedral door? But sir, there are several hundred cathedrals in the city. Oh yes, the great cathedral, between the two great towers. Oh, then like the best of men, Mr. Cruncher, off you go to the posting house, to make the change!

MME. DEFARGE. The wife of Evremonde. Where is she?

MISS PROSS. (*Gasps.*) You!

MME. DEFARGE. You know who I am?

MISS PROSS. From your appearance, you might be the wife of Lucifer. Nevertheless, you shall not get the better of me. I am an Englishwoman!

MME. DEFARGE. I've come to pay my compliments to madame. Tell her that I wish to see her.

MISS PROSS. I know that your intentions are evil. And you may depend upon it, I'll hold me own against them.

MME. DEFARGE. It will do her no good to keep herself concealed from me at this time. Good patriots will know what that means. Tell her that I wish to see her!

MISS PROSS. No, you wicked foreign woman! I'm your match!

MME. DEFARGE. Woman, imbecile and pig-like, either tell your mistress that I wish to see her, or stand aside and let me pass.

MISS PROSS. (*Defending the closet door.*) Never! I'm a Briton and I'm desperate! I don't care an English tuppence for myself, but I know that as long as I keep you here, the greater hope there is for my lady-bird. I'll not leave a patch of that dark hair on your head if you so much as lay a finger on me!

MME. DEFARGE. You miserable wretch! What are you worth? I address myself to the Doctor. Citizen Doctor! Wife of Evremonde! Child of Evremonde! Answer me, the Citizeness Defarge! This room is all in disorder. (*Glancing into basket.*) There has been hurried packing. There is nobody behind that door. Stand aside! Let me pass!

MISS PROSS. Never!

MME. DEFARGE. I've been in the street from the start. No one has ever stood in my way! I will tear you to pieces, but I will have you from that door!

MISS PROSS. Have at me, Frenchie! We're at the top of a high house in a solitary courtyard. We're not likely to be overheard. And I pray God for the bodily strength to keep you here. (*THEY fight.*) No you don't! (*THEY tumble over the couch.*) No! no! (*Legs and other body parts are seen in the struggle behind the couch.*) No. No. No. It's under me arm. (*THEY struggle on the couch, upside down.*) You shall not draw! I'm stronger than you, and I thank God for that! I'll hold you here till one or the other of us faints or dies! (*A gun appears.*) No! Oh God! No! No!

(*THEY struggle with the gun. A shot. A death. One pushes the other's body off, with effort. A shriek.*)

MISS PROSS. (*Gasping, approaching the basket.*) God save the queen!

(*An arm and a hand with a knife appears from within the basket, along with a scream [not Jerry's.] JERRY grabs knife, stabs repeatedly at the arm, which disappears within the basket. JERRY takes off skirts, tosses them into the closet, emerges with a shopping bag and the clothes box.*)

REPUBLICAN OFFICER. Halt! Advanced to be recognized! Your papers! (*Opens box and pulls out wrapping tissue, holds one piece of tissue up examines it.*) Dr. Manette! French! Which is he?

Ah! The good Doctor appears not to be in his right mind. Must be the revolutionary fever. Lucy, his daughter. French. (*Removing sexy dress from box.*) Ah! Wife of Evremonde! (*Putting dress on.*) Well well well, wife of Evremonde! Your husband has an assignation elsewhere. (*Mimes the fall of the blade of the guillotine.*) Pfft! (*Examines another piece of paper.*) Lucy, her daughter. English. (*Examining audience.*) Ah! (*Selecting an audience member, stepping into the audience.*) Come to me, child of Evremonde. (*Has audience member zip up back of dress.*) Kiss me child of Evremonde. (*Kisses audience member, returns to stage.*) You have kissed a good Republican (*Raising can of soda from the kitchen.*) Remember that. (*Drinks.*) It is not a common occurrence in your household. (*Examining another piece of tissue paper.*) Sidney Carton, Englishman. (*Raising and lowering shopping bag.*) Ah! The English advocate appears to be in a swoon. (*Nodding.*) I take you to be Mr. Jarvis Lorry. (*Tossing empty clothes box onto floor behind couch.*) Pass!

LUCY. Can they not be induced to go faster?

MR. LORRY. (*Examining self in dressing table mirror.*) No my dear. It would awaken suspicion.

LUCY. Look back. (*Examining back in mirror.*) Look back and see if we are pursued!

MR. LORRY. No, my dear. The road is clear.

JERRY. (*Throwing tissue paper into wastebasket, sitting at table, applying lipstick, putting on female wig, taking arm-length gloves from drawer, sings softly.*) Take another little piece of my heart now baby!

(*JERRY puts on gloves. A car horn honks. JERRY takes feather boa from shopping bag, wraps it around his shoulders, examines himself in the mirror. Car horn sounds again. JERRY raps on window to acknowledge it. Turns.*)

SEAMSTRESS. Citizen Evremonde, I am the poor seamstress. I was condemned with you on the same day. I've been accused of plots. But is it likely? Who would think of plotting with a poor weak creature like me? I am not afraid to die. The just lord knows that I have done nothing. I am not unwilling to die, if the Republic, which promises to do so much good for the poor, could profit from my death. (*Weeps.*) But I cannot see how that is possible. (*Controls herself.*) Pardon, monsieur. If I may ride with you this afternoon, in the cart, to the guillotine, will you let me hold your hand? I am not afraid to die. It's just ... it's just that I'm weak, and it might give me more courage. (*Gasps.*) But you are not the Citizen Evremonde! Who are you? You're going to die for him? You're going to die in his place? You will let me hold your hand, won't you, brave stranger? (*Reaches hand out to his, grasps it.*)

JERRY. (*Running to dressing table, writing.*) His name is Dorian. I couldn't take care of him. I hope you can. (*Gets keys.*)

SIDNEY. (*Placing note in basket taking it up.*) It's a far far better thing I do than I have ever done. (*Opening door.*) It's a far far greater rest I go to than I have ever known.

(*JERRY exits. Guillotine emerges from the closet in a cloud of smoke. The blade falls. The curtain call music is an upbeat popular tune for lipsynching.*)

Costume Plot

Blue denim jacket trimmed in lace and leather with elaborate buttons. White cotton shirt. Long brown wig tied back.	Blue denim shorts. Open inseam and put in a long zipper (good bit when removing pants.) Pair of combat boots. Layer socks with one pair of heavy opaque stocking rolled down as bottom layer. Can get laugh in strip by pulling one up.
A tricorn hat made of household items. Elaborate 18th century coat. Pair of pajama pants.	Elaborate tricorn hat. Large bath towel. Pair of bedroom slippers. Mob cap.
Pannier skirt made of a bird cage, a hat box, and various things found in a closet. Black corset. Pair of pantyhose.	Pair of black panties. Pair of silver high-heeled shoes.
Pair of red high-heeled shoes. Elaborate skirt which is concealed onstage as the skirt on the dressing table Pair of sequinned evening gloves.	Floor-length quilted dressing coat. Black sequined dress. Red feather boa.

Property Plot

Set of keys.
Large elegant shopping bag.
Six-pack of Coke.
A stack of mail.
A milk crate.
A hideous baby puppet.

Garbage can.
A small dish towel.
Can of hairspray.
Frozen dinner (something with gravy—it makes better steam.
Plate.
1 squeeze ketchup bottle filled with stage blood.
1 large afghan.

A rat tail comb.

Feather.
Large scissors.

Large crystal.
Large bath towel.
Large knife.
Wrapped flowers.
2 bed sheets.
Broom.

Dress box.
Grocery bag.

A box of donuts.
A telephone.
A wrapped baby.
Note pinned to baby blanket.
Roll of paper towels.
Soiled baby diaper.
Hair clasp.
Fork.

1 bent fork.
1 white rose hair clip.

1 pair of large lace work needles or 2 turkey basters.
Several wigs in various stages of being done.
3 large coins.
1 squeeze bottle filled with water.
Radio.
Alarm clock.
Bottle of tranquilizers.
Vase with flowers.
Steak knife.
Can of shaving cream.

Razor.
And aged letter.

Face powder and puff.

Large bell.
Eyebrow pencils.
Jar of cold cream.
Blush.
Plastic water glasses.
Note paper.

A rat trap.
Max Factor pan stick
or equivalent.
Waterproof puppet of
Lucy's daughter.
Eye shadow compact.
Fat eye shadow pencils.
Box of tissues.
A gun.
Lipstick.
A guillotine.

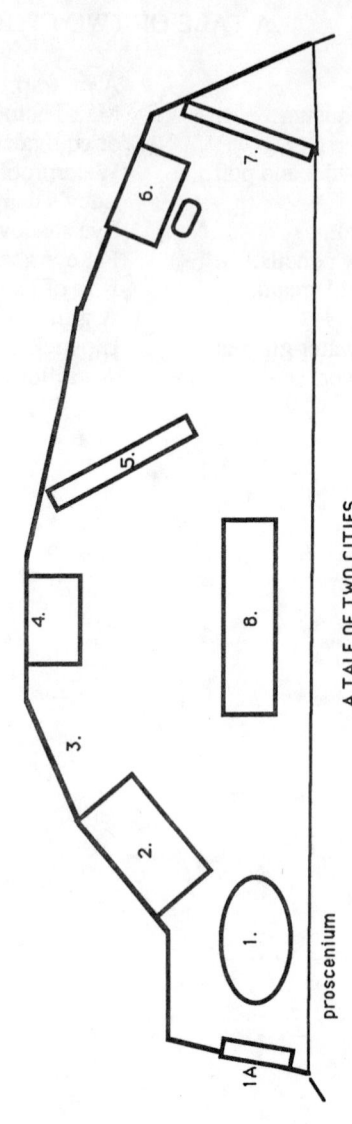

A TALE OF TWO CITIES

1. Working bathtub; 1A. Towel rack; 2. Shelf unit w/working microwave oven and refridgerator; 3. Window with security gate.; 4. Book shelf unit with chest of drawers/cut hole in top of bureau; 5. Door with chain and lock; 6. Vanity, swivel chair and shelves on wall for wig heads; 7. Closet door; 8. Convertible sofa.